AUG 1 4

21st
Century
Skills Library

COOL STEM CAREERS

HYDROLOGIST

JOSH GREGORY

Published in the United States of America by
Cherry Lake Publishing, Ann Arbor, Michigan
www.cherrylakepublishing.com

Content Adviser
Jeffrey McDonnell, PhD, Professor of Hydrology, Global Institute for Water Security,
National Hydrology Research Centre, University of Saskatchewan, Saskatoon,
Saskatchewan, Canada

Photo Credits: Cover and page 1, ©Chris Sattlberger/Media Bakery;
page 4, ©AlexandreNunes/Shutterstock, Inc.; page 6, ©Mariusz S. Jurgielewicz/
Shutterstock, Inc.; page 8, ©Portokalis/Shutterstock, Inc.; page 10, ©Foto011/
Shutterstock, Inc.; page 12, ©Paul Glendell/Alamy; page 15, ©Ashley Cooper/
Alamy; page 16, U.S. Geological Survey; page 18, ©Robert Kneschke/Shutterstock,
Inc.; page 20, U.S. Geological Survey/photo by Kathleen M. Rowland; page 23, U.S.
Geological Survey/photo by Dave Ozman; page 24, U.S. Geological Survey/photo by
Stan Paxton; page 27, ©Justine Evans/Alamy; page 28, U.S. Geological Survey/
photo by K. Scott Jackson.

Library of Congress Cataloging-in-Publication Data
Gregory, Josh.
  Hydrologist/by Josh Gregory.
     p. cm.—(Cool STEM careers) (21st century skills library)
  Audience: Grades 4–6.
  Includes bibliographical references and index.
  ISBN 978-1-62431-001-0 (lib. bdg.) — ISBN 978-1-62431-025-6 (pbk.) —
ISBN 978-1-62431-049-2 (e-book)
  1. Hydrology—Vocational guidance—Juvenile literature. 2. Hydrologists—Juvenile
literature. 3. Vocational guidance--Juvenile literature. I. Title.
  GB662.3.G754 2013
  551.48023—dc23   2012034716

Cherry Lake Publishing would like to acknowledge
the work of The Partnership for 21st Century Skills.
Please visit *www.21stcenturyskills.org* for more information.

Printed in the United States of America
Corporate Graphics Inc.
January 2013
CLSP12

HYDROLOGIST

TABLE OF CONTENTS

CHAPTER ONE
FROM PUDDLES TO OCEANS

J esse opened the refrigerator and took out the pitcher of water. After playing basketball outside on this hot summer day, he was ready for a refreshing drink.

Water is refreshing on a hot day.

His mom smiled as he poured the water into a glass and took a long drink.

"Thirsty?" she asked.

"I sure am," he said, using his arm to wipe sweat from his forehead. "Maybe I should take a shower."

"Good idea," Jesse's mom replied. "Try not to stay in there too long, though. You don't want to waste water."

Jesse set his glass down as a thoughtful expression came over his face. "Hey Mom, where does all this water come from?"

"What do you mean?"

"Well, we have water in the fridge, and there's water in the shower. But I've never seen a lake around here. Our water has to come from somewhere, right?"

"You're right," said Jesse's mom. "We live in a pretty dry area. Luckily, there are scientists and **engineers** who know how to bring the water to us!"

■ ■ ■

Water is one of the planet's most valuable natural resources. People, animals, and plants all need water to survive. We drink it and use it to prepare food. We also use it to clean our possessions and ourselves. Farmers use it to help their crops grow, and companies use it to manufacture products. In the United States alone, people use more than 400 billion gallons (1.5 trillion liters) of water each day.

Water covers about 71 percent of Earth's surface. Without water, life as we know it could not exist. Even the planet's physical features would be different. This is because water is one of the major shapers of Earth's landforms. Roaring rivers help dig deep valleys and canyons in rocky environments. The constant movement of ocean waves wears away the edges of coastlines.

Ocean waves help shape the cliffs along the coastline of central California.

Earth's water supply is limited. The total amount of water on the planet can never increase or decrease. Almost all of Earth's water is saltwater, most of which is located in the world's oceans. People cannot drink this water because our bodies cannot process the high levels of salt.

To survive, people need freshwater. Just 3 percent of the planet's water supply is freshwater. This is the water that rains down from the sky and makes up most rivers, lakes, and ponds. It is also the water that goes into the ground to become groundwater. People drink freshwater and use it for important tasks.

LIFE & CAREER SKILLS

Many people do not stop to consider whether or not they waste water at home. There are many simple ways you can avoid using more water than you need. When you wash your hands, turn off the faucet while you lather the soap. You can also turn off the faucet after wetting your toothbrush to brush your teeth. Avoid using the toilet to flush trash away. Each flush in most toilets uses more than 2 gallons (7.5 L) of water!

Water is constantly moving from the planet's surface to the **atmosphere** and back down again. This process is known as the hydrologic cycle or water cycle. Water falls from clouds in the atmosphere as rain, snow, or other forms of **precipitation**. Some precipitation seeps into the soil to become groundwater. At any given time, about 20 to 30 percent of Earth's freshwater is located underground. Most of the rest of the precipitation collects in rivers, lakes, and other bodies of water.

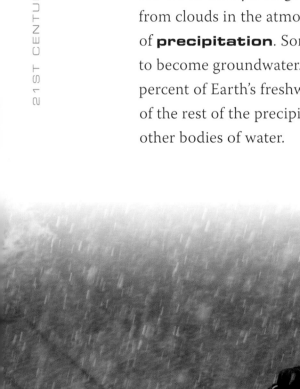

Precipitation can be anything from a light snowfall to a heavy rain shower.

At the same time, water located on Earth's surface **evaporates** into the air. This happens when the water warms, when wind blows, or when the air is dry. Evaporated water turns into a gas called water vapor. The vapor rises into the atmosphere, where it **condenses** into a liquid or solid form, creating clouds. Then it falls back to the ground as precipitation.

Freshwater is plentiful in many parts of the world. But this is not the case everywhere. Some areas are simply very dry. There is little rainfall, and large bodies of surface water are uncommon. Other areas have accessible water, but it is not safe to use for drinking or washing. Sometimes this is because of **pollution** caused by humans. In other cases, the water might contain life-forms such as bacteria or **parasites**, which can make people sick.

Because our water supply is limited, it is important to keep careful track of how we use it. Hydrologists are scientists who study water and the water cycle. They keep a close eye on how water is distributed throughout different parts of the world. They monitor how quickly bodies of water move and how much water is moving from one place to another. They take water and soil samples to determine the quality of water in an area. They also find out how local water supplies are affected by human activities. With this information, they make important decisions about how people should use water supplies in different areas.

Hydrological studies can have a major impact on everything from daily activities in a small town to major international construction projects. Hydrologists might work with homeowners to help prevent rainwater from forming pools in their backyards. They might conduct studies to predict floods or droughts, and help prepare for these disasters. Hydrologists work with engineers to design and build **irrigation** systems that provide water to dry areas.

Some reservoirs created by dams are very large.

Dams are structures that control how much water is allowed to flow into an area. Some dams are designed to collect water into **reservoirs** so people can use it. Other dams take advantage of the movement of rivers to create electricity. Many are designed to slow down floods. Some dams are designed to do all of these things at once. Dams are very useful. But if one is built in the wrong place, it can cause terrible problems for the surrounding wildlife and communities. Before any dam is built, hydrologists study the area carefully. They try to figure out exactly what effects the dam would have.

A wastewater treatment facility is another type of structure that affects our water supply. Anything you pour down the drain of a sink or flush down a toilet ends up at one of these locations. There, this wastewater goes through a process that removes harmful substances. Once the water is clean, it can be released into nearby bodies of water. It might also be used for irrigation. Hydrologists carefully monitor the operations at these facilities to make sure that polluted water does not get into an area's water supply.

Hydrologists sometimes work with companies and governments. They provide knowledge to help these groups create new laws and regulations. For example, if a certain type of pollution is affecting local water samples, hydrologists might find out what is causing the pollution. The scientists then suggest rules to prevent the problem from continuing. They also research ways for companies or communities to use less water.

CHAPTER TWO
INDOORS AND OUTDOORS

Because there are so many uses for water, there are a number of different jobs for hydrologists to do. Some work for private companies. Others are employed by state,

Many hydrologists spend time in the field gathering samples that they will study more closely in a lab later.

local, or federal governments. Depending on where they work, some hydrologists might focus more on planning construction projects. Others might concentrate on improving water quality or increasing water availability in dry areas. No matter whom they work for or what projects they are working on, these scientists usually split their time between fieldwork and office work.

Hydrologists work in the field to get a firsthand look at water supplies. They take samples of the water and the soil so they can test them later. They also use a variety of equipment to measure how fast a body of water is moving, how much precipitation is soaking into the soil, and other important information.

Sometimes fieldwork is as simple as taking a quick drive from the office to a nearby stream. Other times, a hydrologist has to travel to a remote location to get the needed information. For example, some hydrologists specialize in studying **glaciers** located in some of the coldest parts of the world. It can be very difficult for people to travel to these distant locations. There are no airports, towns, or roads near most glaciers. This is also true of some water sources deep in jungles or in mountainous areas.

Because these locations are so difficult to reach, some hydrologists take long trips to do field studies. They hike into dense forests and climb high mountains. Sometimes they do this while carrying heavy equipment for gathering information. The weather can be extreme in these areas. Hydrologists often work in incredibly hot or cold conditions. They might also have to deal with heavy precipitation or fast-moving waters.

21ST CENTURY CONTENT

Melting glaciers have been a major environmental issue in recent years. Almost 70 percent of all freshwater is frozen in glaciers. When glaciers start to melt, this water flows into rivers and oceans and mixes with saltwater. This means the freshwater supply in some areas is slowly decreasing. Melting glaciers also cause ocean levels to rise. This can result in coastal areas disappearing underwater. Such risks make glaciers an important subject for hydrologists to study.

Some hydrologists study how quickly glaciers are melting or try to trace where the melted water flows.

Once hydrologists reach the right location, they might wade into a stream to set up a device that measures the volume of water flow. Or they might drill deep into the center of a glacier to collect an ice sample. Sometimes, a hydrologist simply needs to check a device that was already installed. No matter what hydrologists are doing, they keep careful and detailed records of their findings. Like any other branch of science, hydrology depends on collecting precise, accurate information.

Hydrologists usually head back to their offices or laboratories after collecting the information they need. The work they do indoors is very different from what they do outside.

They run tests and perform experiments on the samples they collected in the field. They might then compare their findings with older hydrological studies to see how things are changing. This could involve looking up the information in books or Internet resources. They might also create graphs of their findings. Graphs make it easier for people who aren't experts in hydrology to understand how an area's water supply changes over time.

Sometimes hydrologists create computer models. These computer programs use current and historical hydrological data to predict what might happen in the future. Hydrologists use these models to look for possible problems before serious

In a laboratory, hydrologists have easy access to the equipment and supplies they need for running tests.

damage occurs. They also use models to predict floods and study how new construction projects or a change in water usage might affect an area over time.

Hydrologists often prepare written reports of their findings. The reports might be written for government officials or business leaders. These people use hydrological reports to make decisions about projects that could affect water supplies. Other reports are written mainly for fellow hydrologists or other scientists. The information in these reports can help the scientists with their own studies.

Some hydrologists work as professors at universities. They make discoveries about certain parts of the hydrologic cycle and develop new ways of measuring things. They create new models to predict possible changes in water quantity and water quality. They conduct field studies and prepare reports just as other hydrologists do. However, they are also responsible for teaching classes and overseeing research projects conducted by their students. They often allow students to assist them in the field with their own projects.

Most hydrologists are employed in full-time positions. However, this doesn't mean they have regular work schedules. Fieldwork sometimes requires them to work very long hours. They might also need to work on weekends or holidays or at odd times of the day. Some projects require weeks away from home to complete. Hydrology is not always an easy job, but it is a rewarding, exciting, and ever-changing one.

CHAPTER THREE
DIVING IN

Hydrologists cannot do their jobs without a deep understanding of water systems and other aspects of the natural world. This means that anyone who wants to become a hydrologist must first get a good education. Students considering a career in hydrology should focus on

Studying for a career in hydrology can be hard work. Teachers and your classmates can help you along the way.

science and math courses. It is also important to develop computer skills.

Hydrologists need to attend college. Most hydrologists have at least a master's degree, which requires a total of around six years of college. Some have a doctorate, which takes a little longer. There are hydrology jobs available for people who have only a bachelor's degree, but a master's degree is required for most positions. Hydrologists who work as university professors always hold a doctorate.

Most universities do not offer undergraduate degrees specifically in hydrology. Instead, students who want to study hydrology get degrees in related fields. Some study **geology** or environmental sciences. Others study civil or environmental engineering. Most future hydrologists take courses in a variety of other topics that will help them with their research. For example, it is common for hydrology students to study math, physics, and statistics. Such knowledge is especially helpful when creating graphs and computer models. They take courses in biology and other life sciences to understand how water affects plants, animals, and other living things. Certain hydrology jobs also require business skills. As a result, many future hydrologists take classes in marketing, economics, and finance. Courses in environmental law can help hydrologists who want to work for the government.

Hydrologists do not get all of their education from books and classrooms. Even as students, they are likely to spend a lot of time doing fieldwork. Professors often bring students with them when conducting their own research. Some students might spend their summer or winter breaks working as assistants to hydrologists. This hands-on experience helps students learn practical skills that they will need in their careers. Because they work under the supervision of

Experience in the field and in the office are important for a person hoping to become a hydrologist.

experts, they can learn and make mistakes without causing serious problems for an area's water supply.

Field training also gives hydrology students a chance to learn how to use advanced equipment. Many hydrologists use a geographic information system (GIS) in their projects. These advanced computer programs allow scientists to gather and access a huge variety of detailed information about an area's landforms and water systems. A GIS offers so much information that it can be difficult for beginners to use. Students must spend time learning how to use these systems.

The global positioning system (GPS) is another important technology for hydrologists to learn about. This system uses satellites to pinpoint exact locations around the world. It is especially useful for **navigation** and mapmaking.

In addition to having a firm understanding of science and technology, hydrologists usually need strong communication skills. They often meet with government and business leaders, other scientists, and members of the public to discuss their findings and ideas. Some hydrologists might be asked to give presentations before large crowds. All hydrologists need to be skilled in written communications. Their written reports need to be clear and easy to understand.

LIFE & CAREER SKILLS

If you're thinking of becoming a hydrologist, one skill that you should start practicing right away is teamwork. Hydrologists rarely work alone. They might conduct fieldwork with a team of assistants, fellow hydrologists, and other scientists. They also work closely with people such as engineers and **architects** to help plan construction projects. Members of a team rely on one another to make sure a job gets done. They must listen to their teammates and respect one another's opinions. These skills are useful not just in hydrology, but in many other careers as well.

Finally, hydrologists need a variety of skills that can't be learned in a classroom. They must be able to think critically and come up with solutions to difficult problems. Hydrologists working in the field need the physical strength to journey into wilderness areas and work with heavy equipment. Most importantly, they should have a love of the outdoors and a strong appreciation for the natural world.

Some hydrologists speak to reporters about their studies.

CHAPTER FOUR
FLOWING INTO THE FUTURE

Hydrology is one of the fastest-growing professions in the United States. As of 2010, there were around 7,600 people working as hydrologists in the United

Hydrologists who work for the government sometimes help run programs to educate the public.

States. By 2020, that number is expected to increase to around 9,000. Today, about 30 percent of all hydrologists work directly for the U.S. government. Government agencies such as the U.S. Geological Survey, the Environmental Protection Agency, the National Weather Service, the Bureau of Land Management, and the U.S. Forest Service all employ hydrologists. Another 20 percent work for state and local governments. Architecture and engineering companies employ around 22 percent of all hydrologists. The remaining 28 percent work for a variety of other private companies. As environmental responsibility continues to become a greater priority in the world, more private organizations are expected to hire hydrologists to help plan their activities.

Experts predict that hydrologists with advanced computer skills are the most likely to find success in the job market in coming years. Like many careers, hydrology is relying more and more on technology. Those who keep up to date with the latest technological developments will have a strong advantage over the competition.

As of May 2010, most hydrologists earned around $76,000 per year. The highest-paid hydrologists can earn more than $112,000, while the lowest paid can make less than $48,000 per year. Hydrologists employed by the U.S. government or certain private organizations tend to make more than those who work for state or local governments. For example, in 2010 the average U.S. government hydrologist earned over $20,000 more than most state government hydrologists.

LEARNING & INNOVATION SKILLS

Earth's human population is increasing at a rapid rate. Unfortunately, the planet's water supply does not increase along with the number of people. This means that as time goes on, there will be less freshwater water available to each person. If we continue to use water at the same rate we do now, there simply won't be enough to go around. Hydrologists will be among those tasked with finding new ways to make sure that our water supply is able to meet the needs of the growing population. They will need to use their skills and knowledge to think outside the box if they hope to solve this issue.

Climate change is a major environmental issue that will continue to affect our planet in the future. Precipitation patterns and temperatures are expected to change significantly in coming years. Such changes can lead to devastating droughts and floods. Hydrologists must work to protect against the harmful effects of these disasters.

Hydrology can involve dangerous work—like descending deep into gaps in a glacier!

Hydrologists play an important role in the quest to keep our planet healthy. Their work helps us find ways to conserve resources for future generations. One day, you could be a hydrologist helping protect Earth from environmental disasters. Being a hydrologist isn't easy, but it could lead to the greatest reward of all: a healthy planet where people can continue to thrive.

Hydrologists helped in the construction of the Crown Fountain in Chicago, Illinois.

SOME WELL-KNOWN HYDROLOGISTS

Daniel Bernoulli (1700–1782) was a Swiss scientist who came from a family of mathematicians. He studied a wide range of scientific fields, including biology, physics, and astronomy. His most famous discoveries concern how liquids flow from one area to another. His work remains an important part of hydrological studies today.

Henry Darcy (1803–1858) was an engineer whose research led to the discovery of what became known as Darcy's law, which describes how water flows underground. Darcy's law is used for research in hydrology and many other scientific fields.

Pierre Perrault (ca. 1611–1680) was a French hydrologist who proved the existence of the hydrologic cycle. Many earlier scientists did not believe that enough precipitation fell in a single area to keep its rivers and streams from drying up. Perrault found that the amount of water flowing out of a river was far less than the amount of precipitation that fell over an area. This proved that precipitation could easily keep the area's waterways flowing.

Charles Vernon Theis (1900–1987) created mathematical equations that predicted the results of pumping water out of underground sources known as aquifers. These equations revolutionized the way hydrologists thought about using underground water sources.

GLOSSARY

architects (AHR-kuh-tekts) people who design and draw plans for buildings

atmosphere (AT-muhs-feer) the mixture of gases that surrounds a planet

climate (KLYE-mit) the weather typical of a place over a long period of time

condenses (kuhn-DEN-siz) turns from a gas into a liquid

engineers (en-juh-NEERZ) people who design and build machines or large structures such as bridges and roads

evaporates (i-VAP-uh-rayts) changes into vapor or gas

geology (jee-AH-luh-jee) the study of the earth's physical structure, especially its soil and rock

glaciers (GLAY-shurz) slow-moving masses of ice

irrigation (ir-uh-GAY-shuhn) the practice of supplying water to crops by artificial means

navigation (nav-uh-GAY-shuhn) the practice of planning a route

parasites (PAR-uh-sites) plants or animals that live on or inside another plant or animal, depending on it to survive

pollution (puh-LOO-shuhn) harmful materials that damage or contaminate the air, water, and soil

precipitation (pri-sip-uh-TAY-shuhn) water that falls from the sky in the form of rain, sleet, hail, or snow

reservoirs (REZ-ur-vwahrz) natural or artificial lakes in which water is collected and stored for use

FOR MORE INFORMATION

BOOKS

Benduhn, Tea. *Water Power*. Pleasantville, NY: Weekly Reader Publishing, 2009.

Gardner, Robert. *Water: Green Science Projects for a Sustainable Planet*. Berkeley Heights, NJ: Enslow Publishers, 2011.

Taylor-Butler, Christine. *Hydrology: The Study of Water*. New York: Children's Press, 2012.

WEB SITES

EPA—Water Trivia Facts
http://water.epa.gov/learn/kids/drinkingwater/water_trivia _facts.cfm
Check out some interesting facts about Earth's water supply.

Garmin—What Is GPS?
www8.garmin.com/aboutGPS
Learn more about how the global positioning system works.

USGS—Where Is Earth's Water Located?
http://ga.water.usgs.gov/edu/earthwherewater.html
Learn more about the different types of water found on Earth.

INDEX

ABOUT THE AUTHOR

Josh Gregory writes and edits books for kids. He lives in Chicago, Illinois.